*"ONLY THOSE WHO WILL
RISK GOING TOO FAR
CAN POSSIBLY FIND OUT
HOW FAR ONE CAN GO"*

T. S. Eliot

Disclaimer & Copyright:

Front and back cover graphic design and layout by:
Michelle Giacchetta
President of MAG Designs Syracuse, New York

Published by:
Buffalo Road Imports, LLC
10120 Main Street
Clarence, NY 14031, USA
www.BuffaloRoadImports.com

Printed in USA

Northwest Engineering Company

A Photographic Archive collection

Volume One

The First and Second Generation machines 1920 to 1940

Photographic compiling, text, and editing by: M.E Folsom & M. J Torres

(Above) A shipment of Northwest Engineering Company's Model 2 cranes being readied at the factory in Green Bay Wisconsin in 1929. From 1920 to 1940 Northwest would ship to customers worldwide 6166 machines, making it possible for the company to proudly proclaim in their sales literature of the period "The world's largest exclusive builders of gasoline, electric and Diesel powered shovels, cranes, draglines, pullshovels and skimmer scoops."

(Front cover) A Northwest Model 104 shovel loads out the very first type of mobile hauling units available to contractors a team of dependable mules pulling a sturdy wooden bottom dump wagon. One can only speculate at what the contractor or be it the jobsite foreman might be thinking standing watching. Perhaps it was "This new Northwest is the only way to dig".

Table of Contents

Introduction

This photographic picture volume is meant to complement the previous published work of Mario Torres and myself entitled *"Manufactured at Green Bay, Wisconsin, The Story of Northwest Engineering Company."* The reason for a photographic archive book is two-fold. First, the images that Mr. Torres and I had unearthed and received during the research phase of our previous work was so immense that it was impossible to include them into the first book. Secondly, when one thinks of machinery produced by Northwest, images of "pekin" orange and black shovels, pullshovels, and draglines come to mind, not to mention the streamlined rounded house designs of the mid-1950's and then later, the Series II upgraded machines. There were three whole generations of machines that came beforehand that helped usher in those later magnificent machines. This is the foundation to a legend that should not be forgotten, for had it not been for these early incarnations, devotees of Northwest would not see the sightings of 'pekin orange "we have come so much to enjoy.

The story has been told, but to quote English rock musicians Rod Stuart and Ronnie Wood, *"every picture tells a story"*. Words are powerful, but a good photograph can communicate what we as writers try to get across in pages of paragraphs. That is not meant to detract from one's ability to provoke illusion by the reader on the subject at hand, but when imagery is available, very little in the way of declarations are needed. Some of the images within this book have been illustrated in the prior publication, however these images are important and vital photographs to help start, tell and complete a photographic work of this nature. To leave them out would somehow narrow the opus.

This is the first in a series of photographic archive collection publications pertaining to Northwest's classic construction equipment lines. To quote yet another musician Randy Buchman; *"you ain't seen nothin' yet"*.

Enjoy,

M.E. Folsom

Acknowledgments

There are a few individuals who deserve acknowledging for this archive taking form. To start with two good friends of ours, Mr. Alan Brickett and Mr. Edgar Browning. Mr. Brickett was a mechanical engineer for Northwest who joined the company in the early 1950's. His interview for that said position deserves to be mentioned as a testament to his own ingenuity. As a mechanical engineering student at Tufts University in Boston, Mr. Brickett built a working scale model of a Northwest Model 25-T truck crane in his junior year. This model was fully functional with small electric motors providing all the needed power for movement. The model was subsequently shown and demonstrated at the school's engineering department's annual open house. The New England sales representative from Northwest by the name of Martin Brennan was in attendance at that show and quizzed Mr. Brickett on how he came to build such a model of a Northwest machine. Mr. Brickett replied that his father had an assortment of Northwest sales literature and that he thought it would be fun to build a model of a Model 25-T truck crane. So impressed was he with the young engineering student's efforts, that Mr. Brennan told Mr. Brickett to contact the Northwest engineering department for possible employment; following a brief telephone interview he was offered an intern engineering position at Northwest that coming summer. The following year after graduation, then chief engineer at Northwest Edward Blanchard offered him a permanent engineering position.

Mr. Brickett remained with Northwest until his retirement in 1981, working his way up to the head engineer of special projects for the company. A self-admitted "pack rat" he indeed had the opportunity to scrounge up various records and artifacts of his company over the years. The real treasure trove came near the end of his tenure at Northwest. One day he spotted some of the photographic archives being boxed up and placed curbside for disposal. At the end of the day he pulled his station-wagon up along the curb and loaded up what was approximately 45 years of company photographs. The vast majority of the following collections of images are from Mr. Brickett's curbside haul. Thank you, Alan.

Renowned heavy equipment photographic archivist and author Edgar Browning was responsible for the majority of the image scanning. Mr. Browning indeed suffered long hours scanning each of Mr. Brickett's photographs to make this publication even possible. His expertise in image restoration and general knowledge of publication made this sophomore effort of ours a relaxed experience.

Next we must credit; the many unknown photographers of these wonderful images, we are truly indebted to all of them. It is not known if they were employees of the Russell T. Gray Company of Chicago, Northwest's longtime advertising firm who had assembled all of those lavish product catalogs, or hired local photographers located in Green Bay or indeed Northwest employees, but whomever you individuals were, "Thank you."

In a few short years, 2020 to be exact, it will be 100 years since Northwest Engineering Works first set out to capture the crane and excavator market. Even though the company under the guise of Northwest Engineering Company, and four different owners would only last for 70 years building these machines (1990 being the last official year at Green Bay), Northwest would leave their mark. One could hardly pass by a construction job from the 1940's to the 1970's and not see a "pekin orange and black" Northwest doing its thing making their owners profits.

The machines that Northwest devotees have come to admire so much will never be just another crane, dragline, shovel, or a back-hoe (or more correctly in Northwest's idiom "*a pullshovel*"); they are truly works of mechanical genius and heavy equipment architecture. This photographic archive is a statement and an acknowledgment to you the enthusiast that these machines should never, nor will they ever, be forgotten. Neither should the individuals that made the whole endeavor possible, the employees of Northwest.

Lastly, but certainly not least, we wish to thank you, the enthusiast/fan of Northwest Engineering Company and its products. We sincerely hope that you find this work a valuable addition to your library, and keeps the memory of a great company alive.

M.E. Folsom & M. J. Torres

This work is dedicated to Remy' Martin;

Thank you for saving my life by making the bloody stuff so expensive!!

M.E Folsom

Chapter One

"The experimental model and first generation machines"

When the brothers H.G and L.H. Barkhausen decided divest their business of tugboat building and enter the mobile crane and excavator manufacturing field, their company Northwest Engineering Works was poised on the precipice of revolutionary excavating machine ideas and manufacturing techniques. One of the most important concepts the brothers Barkhausen, and that of their chief engineer Paul Burke would bring forth to the enterprise, was that of reliable motive power. Northwest machines would eclipse the steam era of full slew revolving excavators that were still prevalent at the onset of the 1920's. Gasoline power equipment offered reliability and relative ease of maintenance for the operator and owner, plus the economic advantages, and a winning endeavor started to take root. The other major prerequisite for design required by the Barkhausens was freedom from rails. Some machines of this era still relied on rails to support the draw-works. L.H's insistence that their new mobile crane be free to move about via a crawler type of undercarriage was a foreshadowing of things to come.

These new concepts would manifest themselves in the first machine produced: the experimental model. There were also a number of other innovations that engineer Paul Burke would bring forth; the most important of these was for the ease of operation for the operator. Two pioneering patents on Northwest machines put the company's products years ahead of the competition. The first was the ability for the machine to turn its crawler undercarriage with the upper machinery platform in any position. Revolving excavators did not have this ability in the early days of their inception. Burke's idea was simple and rugged. In fact when this idea was presented to the Barkhausen brothers and explained that crawler cranes of the day could not steer this way, they immediately made arrangements to have Paul Burke board a train for Washington, DC and file a patent at the United States Patent office. So great was this concept that it remained the primary style of steering of a Northwest crawler machine for the next eighty years.

The second innovation was for a servo mechanism that would help the operator with the control of the drum clutches. Throwing the long levers to engage the clutches of the hoist or crowd drums was intense work all day long. "Feather-Touch" clutch control, as the innovation would become to be known as, was an immense relief to the long hours of standing that the operator had to endure. Speaking of standing to work a machine of this nature; it was a common sight in the early 1920's to see an operator doing just that: standing. In 1922, Paul Burke added a simple steel saddle seat for the operator to feel a bit more relaxed. Countless operators no doubt have been saying "thank you" ever since.

After the experimental model had proven itself, the first generation machines began production, starting with the Model 104 of one and one quarter cubic yard capacity. It was introduced as a crane in 1921, next introduced, also in 1921, was the smaller 105, of one cubic yard capacity. The Model M, a dragline, followed with longer crawlers and expanded reach in 1924.

A brief distribution of how the Northwest Type M machine evolved is worth citing here to lend insight to chief engineer Paul Burke's acuity to engineering dilemmas. Mr. Burke had among his various duties in the early years of the company the added task of calling on prospective customers that would require more engineering expertise than the average sales person representing Northwest could offer. A situation such as this came about in late 1923 when the city of St. Louis put out to bid a contract to supply new mobile crawler cranes outfitted for dragline duties for maintenance work on the extensive network of levees in and around the city. A meeting was set with the head of city purchasing and various manufactures that could cater to specifications set forth by the engineering department of St. Louis. According to Adrienne Burke Schmitz, Paul Burke's daughter, this meeting took place at a hotel in St. Louis. Burke with other representatives from other crane manufacturers were all gathered in an anti-room off a conference meeting room. Burke having the shrewdness positioned himself to be one of the last representatives to be interviewed. One by one the salesmen conversed with the public officials and as many of them exited with a contemptuous sigh of "no sale" Burke quizzed them as to what was being asked for. Many rebuffed with "it hasn't been made yet" and stormed off. A few of the lesser astute salesmen gave Burke bits of information that he jotted down and started to transform into sketches in his notebook. This machine in rough draft form was even assigned a model type. From the specifications on the prerequisite to bid the contract, and information gathered, Burke calculated the municipality was looking for a dragline equipped machine with an extended reach, greater ability for flotation in soft surface conditions and the capability for an extended work period. By taking the standard Northwest Model 104 dragline equipped machine and modifying it to what the customer needed the Model Type M was born.

When it came time for Paul Burke to answer questions on what Northwest could offer the city, he had the responses that were being sought. Northwest won the contract to supply the new type machines, but more importantly, the company had a rapid academic on their staff to make such transactions possible. When asked back in Green Bay by then company Secretary L.E. Houston; "Burke how did you do"? The chief engineer's droll reply was a humble "all set". This was Paul Burke personified.

Other innovations from Paul Burke would spring fourth in these developing years at Northwest Engineering. The two attachments that would become the biggest sellers on Northwest machines, the first rack-less wire rope crowding front shovel, and a revolutionary adaptation of an attachment for below grade and trench digging, the pullshovel, would propel Northwest to forefront of construction sized full revolving excavators. ***Innovation was a Paul Burke ingrained trait.***

Building a product and promoting it are two different entities. Northwest would work hard and excel at both. The factory in Green Bay was set up with all the latest equipment for the manufacture of crawler cranes and excavators. To quote a Northwest sales catalog of the period: "The Northwest Engineering Company's plant is the latest devoting its entire effort to the manufacture of gasoline and electric shovels, cranes, draglines, pull shovels and skimmer scoops exclusively, and is complete in every essential. Jigs and fixtures are used to an extent heretofore unknown in this industry, resulting in positive interchangeability of parts. Low cost of production and workmanship of a superior quality. Even a special heat treating plant has been installed for the purpose of heat treating the more important parts. " With the entire machine being manufactured in one place (less its supplied power-plant), the company would claim to offer a superior product not found with other manufacturers who offered similar merchandise adapted from several machines types for reasons of economy.

The first promotional showings of the new Northwest products came in 1922 at the Chicago Road Show. A Model 104 with serial number 215 was equipped with the new shovel front and presented; this machine immediately garnered much attention in the construction industry. In the coming years many promotional showings would occur, but Northwest Engineering would also invest wisely in the production of fairly lavish sales catalogs to promote their line. These highly collectable catalogs produced by the Russell T. Gray Company of Chicago Illinois would help the growing sales forces educate the perspective customer for years to come.

Keen innovations, craftsmanship of a product with good promotion and sensible product pricing, were a guaranteed formula for success.

Now the journey begins:

The Northwest Engineering Works experimental model is seen here at the firm's plant located in Green Bay, Wisconsin. Built in 1920 to test the merits of company owners H.G Barkhausen and L.H. Barkhausen's ideas, chief engineer Paul Burke set out with the creed from L.H. "To build a machine for service and not for sale." L.H Barkhausen wanted the best possible combination of performance and reliability .The company would work the experimental model for over a year testing its designs and innovations for any weaknesses or flaws; none were found. Even this very first machine built, with gasoline power, displayed a clean, purposeful appearance. Notice the manufacturer's name on the roof, and the proud name "NORTHWEST" on the counterweight, which would grace the counterweights of future machines Northwest would produce.

To quote Paul Burke "people liked the looks of our machines".

The Northwest Engineering Works experimental model shown here is put to work with an electromagnet on drop ball work at the Northwest yard. The experimental model was put to work on many different assignments to prove its reliability and work out mechanical details for future models. Early crane booms of the period were made of steel channels with cross-bracing.

The Northwest Engineering Works experimental model on parade through the streets of Green Bay. People line the sidewalks to watch the spectacle as the machine trundles by. The machine was moved under its own power after assembly at the Northwest plant to the F. Hurbutt coaling facilities at the north end of Green Bay on the east side of the Fox River.

Northwest Model 104, Model 105 & Model Type M

(Model 104) Produced from 1920 to 1929 1-1/4 cubic yard capacity, 22.000 lbs. lift capacity @ 15ft. radius, 64,000 lbs. working weight, gasoline and electric power options

(Model 105) Produced from 1921 to 1929 1 cubic yard capacity, 24,000 lbs. capacity @ 12 ft. radius, 55,000 lbs. working weight, with gasoline and electric power options

(Model Type M) Produced from 1924 to 1929 1-1/4 cubic yard capacity, 24,000 lbs. lift capacity @ 15 ft. radius, 68,000 lbs. working weight, with gasoline and electric power options

A side view of an early production Model 104 crane stands beside the railroad siding in the snowy yard at the Northwest Engineering Company yard in Green Bay Wisconsin. Circa 1920

This Northwest, a Model 104 crane with clamshell bucket, handles hot cement clinker at the South Dakota State Cement Plant in Rapid City, South Dakota. These early cranes had channel booms. Another distinctive feature was the large flap over the boom hoist cables. Note the absence of the tail-plate insignia of Northwest. Item of note, the first production Northwest machines were marketed as Northwest Locomotive Cranes, no model designation was assigned to the units until late 1920. The reason for this was to bring model differentiation between the models being produced and a newer smaller capacity model that would be shortly introduced. Thus the designation of Models 104 and 105 was created.

A Model 104 crane and orange-peel bucket with a lattice boom works on a sewer job. The lattice construction permitted a lighter yet strong boom, allowing for longer lengths than the previous channel-style boom. Also of note is the gear case that encloses the gear drive from the engine to the draw works. Note the large flap over the boom hoist cables.

Top picture shows a latticed boom Model 105 crane loading a Mack AC dump truck. Bottom picture, a new model from Northwest, a Model M dragline works while a steam-powered Marion works beyond. The Model M sports a lattice boom and extended gantry, a first for universal excavators. Note the extended boom for greater reach.

Top, a close-up of the open cab of the Model M shows the extended gantry to reduce boom compression. Also note how the radiator fan was driven by a belt located outside the radiator. Bottom, a Model M loads light ash into high-sided railcars.

The prelude to the Northwest Model Type M machine is seen here with this early dragline equipped Model 104. Note the absence of the operator's seat "necessity is the mother of invention." When your company needs to operate longer shifts and refueling might pose problems: why not add on a deck to the back of a stock machine and lash on drums to act as extra fuel storage. Such was the case for the Palo Verde Irrigation district of Blythe, California. One can only speculate if chief engineer Paul Burke had seen this photograph prior to his visit to St. Louis. No doubt his keen perception to the municipality's bid specifications won Northwest the contract and ushered in a new era of machine design. His recollection of this machine might have been the catalyst to his thought process.

Two views of Northwest cranes working in New York City, dismantling the older elevated railways that operated using small steam tank locomotives known as Forneys. The work takes place amidst a bustling scene on 42nd Street in the top photo, while work takes place on another portion along the same street in the lower picture.

Another Model 104 crane equipped with an orange-peel bucket excavating for an urban renewal project of the 1920's. This view, similar to the one showed on page 17, depicts a number of Model 104's performing trench excavation in this fashion which was a common sight prior to the introduction of a purpose built attachment for the full revolving excavator for digging trenches. This photograph graced the cover of Mr. Horace Lucas' chronicle regarding Northwest that he assembled back in 1995 entitled "Just the Beginning". It was first published in the very last issue of Northwest Engineering's trade journal Material Handling Illustrated dated as the third quarter of 1981.

Courtesy of Horace Lucas. Author's note Mr. Horace Lucas passed away on April 15th 2014 at 98 years of age. He was very instrumental in the publication of the author's previous work. He will be missed by his family, and friends.

Two views of the first generation Model 104 shovel. This first shovel design utilized twin dipper sticks placed within the boom. Also take notice of the heavy riveted nature of the boom.

In the early days of powered earthmoving, the loading technology was well advanced before the hauling methods, as evidenced by the Model 104 shovel loading the horse-drawn wagon. Hauling technology was catching up; however, as seen in the lower picture, as a Best crawler tractor pulls two bottom dump wagons being loaded by the Model 104 shovel. These early Northwest machines had open-sided cabs. At least these operators had a seat!

Another *"necessity is the mother of invention"* application to a machine. The above photographs show two Model 104's originally equipped as shovels. Take off the dipper stick and you can convert to a short swing radius crane with a larger capacity for clamshell work, although the snow being handled in the bottom photograph can hardly be considered a weight challenge. The curtains on the lower machine are partially closed to ward off the cold weather.

Part of Northwest's early marketing programs was ease of their machines to the contractor / owner for transport. Hopefully, the seemingly top-heavy shovel in the top picture is adequately secured on the lowboy. The shovel in the bottom picture is properly secured for rail travel.

Promotion of equipment also set Northwest Engineering Company apart from other manufacturers of friction based revolving excavating equipment. The company would recognize early the power of a good catalog image as in the top photograph, and the value of product promotion at trade shows as depicted in the bottom photograph. These two marketing strategies helped establish Northwest as a leader early on in their industry.

Not all end users of Northwest machines required them to be gasoline powered. Many quarry operations had their own electric generation systems. A Northwest machine could come equipped with a choice of an AC powered motor for all operations.

The first practical below grade revolving digging machine. Chief Engineer Paul Burke is responsible, more so than anyone, for the advancement in the development of the cable backhoe. This novel version had a unique pivoting bucket that allowed dumping from any position. Holding the boom with the hoist cable and using a rack on the boom to lock the stick in relation to the boom, then slackening the drag cable, the bucket could swing down to dump its contents.

An engineering model for an improved pullshovel with a new distinctive "gooseneck" boom. The new design was based on the Model 104. Note how the drag cable padlock sheave was attached to the lower front of the bucket, and the twin sheaves on the side of the boom.

An early Northwest pullshovel goes about its business doing what it was designed to do: efficiently digging a trench. This scene took place at the Northwest plant in Green Bay.

Two pullshovels busy on the job. These machines, with their unique gooseneck booms, cut a distinctive profile. While the Model 104 has the open-side machinery deck, the bottom Model 105 sports a homemade wooden fully-enclosed house.

The stoutness of the Northwest pullshovel is evident here. Heavy, riveted structures predated later welded members in the 1920s. This pullshovel, equipped with a drop-bottom bucket, digs while workers sans hardhats stand around watching. An open trench such as this would never be permitted today without shoring!!

Two Northwest Model 104's working for The Biggs Construction Company of Akron Ohio. Trenching was performed by the 104 pullshovel while ditch clean-up and pipe setting was completed by the 104 equipped with the gooseneck crane boom and clamshell. Such booms aided in the setting of pipe with low overhead conditions as evident in the photograph. (See page 42 for this style crane boom being used to set pipe) Even at this early stage in the company's existence, special circumstances could be met by the exceptional engineering staff with specialized equipment. Note the Schramm steel wheeled air compressor standing idle next to the utility pole.

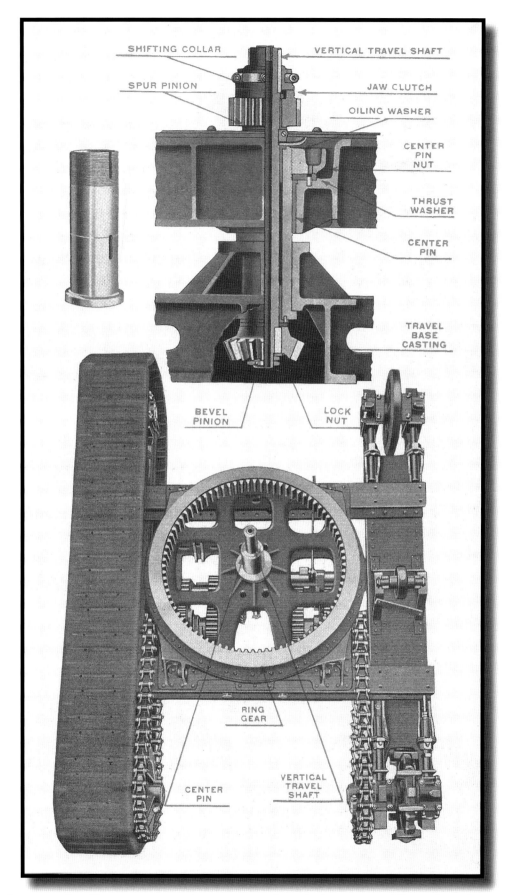

Early Northwest sales literature was instrumental to their success. These brochures were richly illustrated with detailed features highlighting their mechanical superiority to the competition. Here, details of the center pin and vertical shaft for travel are shown.

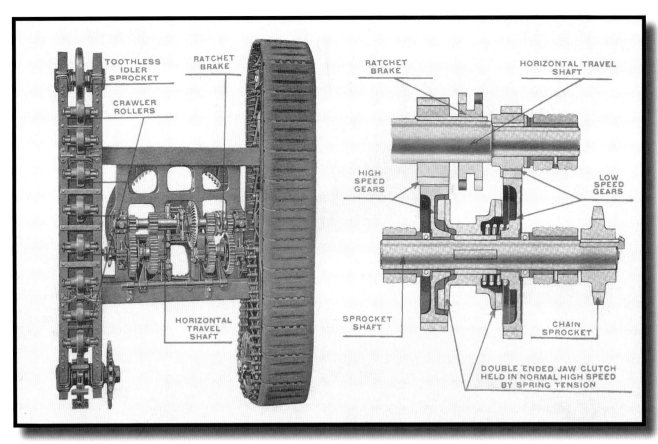

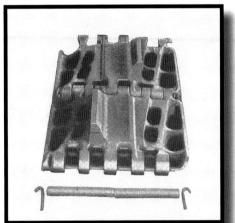 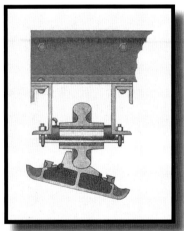 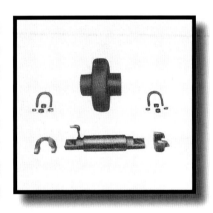

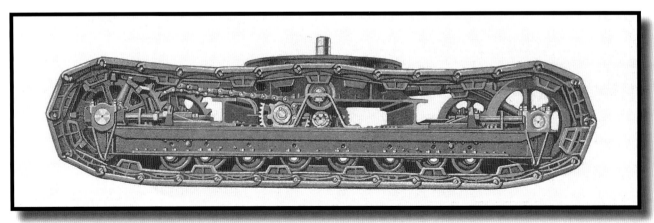

More mechanical details show the lower works. Here, details of the two-speed travel gearing, pivoting crawler pads that allowed rocks and dirt to be shed as well as to relieve stress to reduce pad breakage, and support rollers are shown.

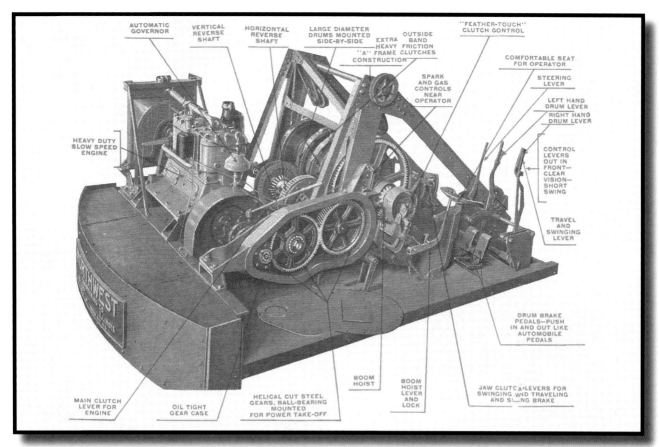

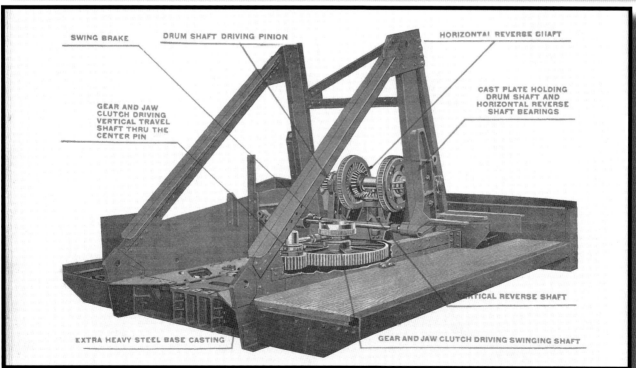

These views, taken from Northwest sales literature, illustrate the machinery deck layouts for the Models 104 and 105. Of note, in the upper picture, is the geared, rather than chain, drive from the engine to the draw works. Also in evidence, is the "Feather-Touch" clutch control designed by Chief Engineer Paul Burke, which made operation easier for the operator. The lower picture shows an early version of the "Uniform Pressure" swing / travel clutch (labeled "horizontal reverse shaft"). The horizontal gears, with the shifter for either swing or travel are also seen. Note the wooden planking used in the model 104 and 105 for deck material.

EXTENDED GANTRY IS STANDARD EQUIPMENT ON MODEL 104 ONLY

PRESSED STEEL REAR DOORS CAN BE LOCKED OPEN OR SHUT

OPERATOR'S WINDOW FOLDS SLIDES DOWN INTO STEEL HALF DOOR WHICH CAN BE SWUNG AND LOCKED IN PLACE ON SIDE OF CAB. OPERATOR HAS UNOBSTRUCTED FRONT AND SIDE VIEW

MACHINE COMPLETELY HOUSED FOR OPERATING IN BAD WEATHER OR LOCKED WHEN NOT IN USE

A big improvement came in the form of a fully-enclosed environment for the operator and machinery deck. Previously, an open-sided cab, with roll-down curtain sides offered at best minimal protection. No doubt, an all-steel cab made a huge difference in operator comfort and machinery protection from the elements.

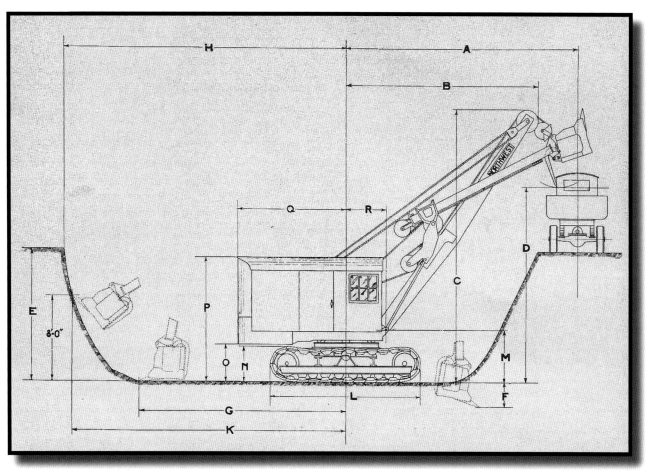

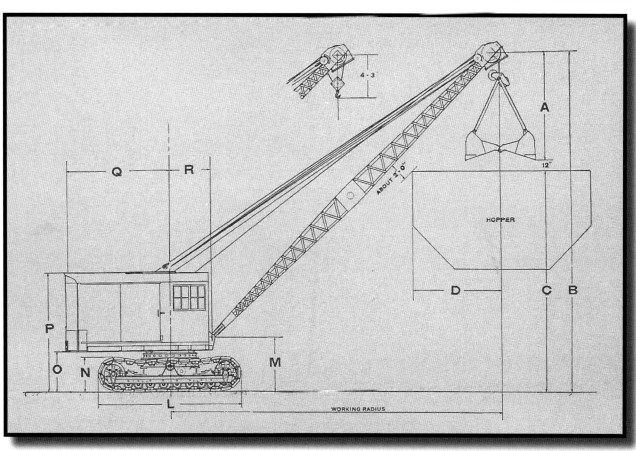

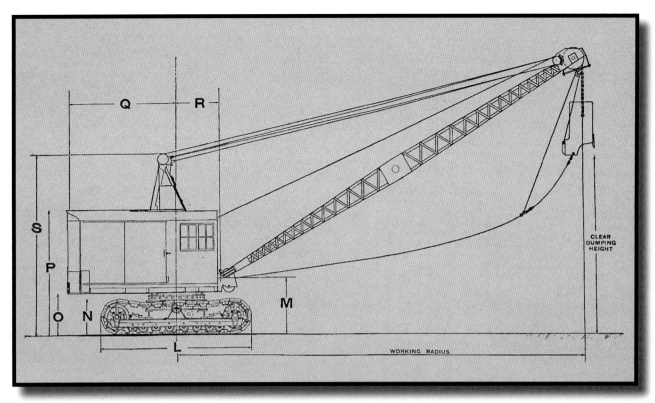

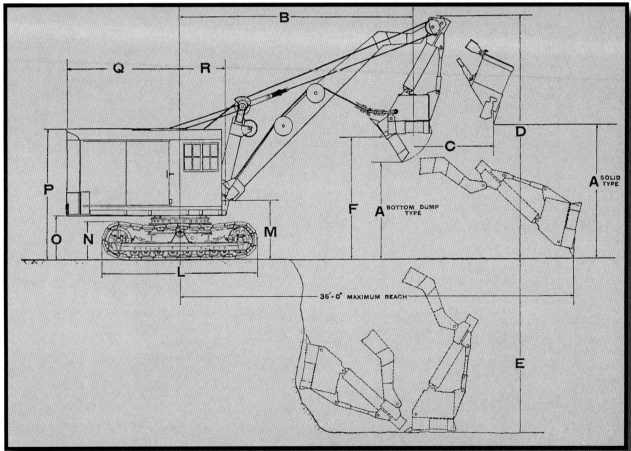

Examples on this and preceding page of range diagrams for the Models 104, Model 105, and the later Model M in various configurations of shovel, crane with clamshell, dragline, and pullshovel with either standard or drop-bottom buckets.

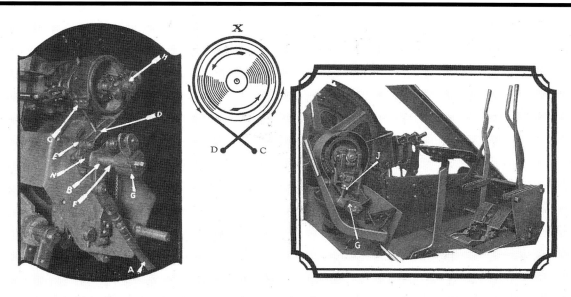

Making handling easy—
the "feather-touch" clutch control

UNCOMFORTABLE operating conditions are not conducive to speed in the handling of machinery.

A bank of many levers that must be pulled through a long arc is confusing, brake pedals that are not in line with operating levers are misleading—and when these work stiffly and tax an operator's strength, anything but speed can be expected. It's a simple case of common sense and the Northwest Engineering Department has made every effort and taken every step possible to promote easy operation, with the result that the Northwest is the easiest handling machine of its type in the field.

By means of the "feather-touch" clutch control, the heavy work of shifting clutches is thrown on the engine, and yet the feel of the operation is retained.

Through the operation of the regular hand lever the power of the engine is utilized to engage the clutch. It is extremely sensitive and is instantaneous in action.

By this unique device all the heavy muscular effort of moving operating levers is eliminated, giving the operator every opportunity for speed. The mechanism is very simple, consisting of a small drum mounted on each end of the drum shaft. Around this drum is a band similar to a brake band which is drawn down on the drum (X) by the pulling of the operating lever.

Following out the operation on the key pictures will show clearly the method of its operation.

When the operator pulls the hand lever the reach rod A moves upward, swinging rocker lever B to the left. This puts a slight tension on the end of band at C, throwing the band into frictional contact with the drum which is revolving to the left. Naturally, then, this pulls on end D of the band. This throws rocker lever E to the right and as both rocker levers E and G are keyed to the same shaft, the movement of one moves the other. The movement of G upward naturally forces link J upward, pushing in the shifter rod H engaging the clutch.

In engagement the pressure on the main clutch band is in the same ratio as the pressure applied to the hand lever.

Release is always positive and sure, and eliminates any danger of hoisting the load through the boom.

On the "feather-touch" clutch control the band touches only during the actual instant of engagement and the operator can remove his hand from the lever after engagement has taken place; it is not necessary to hold it there nor is there any danger of burning up the bands because of friction. In addition to the ease which the clutch control brings there is the general arrangement of the controls, themselves, an arrangement designed to further increase the speed of operation. The arc of the levers is short, the brake pedals work in and out like the clutch and brake of an automobile and are in line with the clutch levers with which they act. To add greater comfort, every Northwest is equipped with a comfortable seat.

The "Feather-Touch" clutch control was a hallmark of the mechanically operated Northwest machines until the introduction of air controls in the early 1960s. This page from early Northwest literature descibes the operation of the mechanism.

Two Model 104 cranes with all-steel cabs equipped with purpose built gooseneck booms perform lifting duties. Note the lattice boom on the bottom machine placing pipe. It also used the clamshell bucket lying nearby, as seen in a previous illustration.

This later Model 105 dragline is excavating out a cut for a storm sewer line on the corner of Sixth Avenue and Slauson Street in Los Angles, California for Lasher & Kisselburg Construction Company. Note the Fordson tractor outfitted with aftermarket crawlers supplied by The Tracford Manufacturing Company of San Francisco. The dozer blade is a hand operated Baker backfiller. The dozer operator and the truck driver are possibly discussing where to meet up after work; to have a cold beer. The potbellied gentlemen with the fedora in the foreground might be either Mr. Lasher of Mr. Kisselburg wondering why production isn't more? Certainly not because of a Northwest was being used.

Author's note: Special thanks to author Roger Amato and noted Fordson tractor expert Edward Brezanson for their help in the identification of the above crawler.

On a building construction job in New York City, Model 105 crane with an unusual jib assists a pile driver in preparing to place the pile beneath the Vulcan steam hammer. A guy derrick can be seen beyond.

The Northwest Cable Crowd

(*Patented*)

IN THE patented cable crowd of the Northwest Convertible Shovel lies an answer to one of the problems of shovel designers, that of being able to dig and crowd without the effort of crowding detracting from the power necessary for digging. In a Northwest there is no loss of digging power while crowding.

The arrangement of the cables is simple and direct. Referring to diagram, the hoisting cable "A" runs from the right hand drum under the guide sheave, over the boom point sheave, down around the padlock sheave at the dipper back, up and over a second boom point sheave, and thence down to a wide faced sheave turning freely on the shipper shaft. Two wraps are taken about this wide faced sheave, from where it goes either to a dead end at the inner end of the stick, or around the sheave at the head of the stick, from where it leads to a non-rotating guide sheave on the shipper shaft, where it is dead ended.

The crowd-in cable "B" runs from the left hand drum to a sheave on the shipper shaft, down to a sheave at the dipper stick end casting and back to a stationary sheave on the shipper shaft, where it is dead ended.

It will readily be seen then that by hoisting on cable "A" the dipper is pulled up through the bank and at the same time the hoist cable, pulling on the end of the cable dead-ended at the upper end of the dipper stick, pulls the dipper into the bank.

Thus crowding becomes a part of hoisting, and all the power is utilized in the digging effort and is not divided between two different mechanisms driving the hoisting drum and crowding drum. For this reason, plus the high horsepowered engine, the Northwest shovel has 25% more power at the dipper lip.

For most work, the hoisting cable "A" is dead ended at the inner end of the stick. For stone quarry work, or for hard shallow grading, the two-part line is preferred. This adjustability of the crowding ratio is an exclusive Northwest feature.

In digging, when crowding is desired, it is only necessary to let the cable "B" run out on the drum. Stopping it holds the dipper back and taking up on the cable pulls the dipper out of the bank. It will thus be seen that there is no machinery whatever on the boom except sheaves.

This design eliminates troublesome racks and pinions, boom engines and crowding chains. As the shipper shaft drum runs freely there is no loss to friction and there is not that wearing drag on the shipper shaft bearings which comes with the chain crowd. Big sheaves allow the cable to run easily, minimizing the amount of wear, thus reducing the changing of cables to as few times a year as possible.

The cable crowd is one of Northwest's paramount features and is responsible for the Northwest's having full power behind the dipper clear to the top of the cut and for the unmatched digging power—digging power that is the reason for the replacement of so many other machines in all classes of work by Northwests.

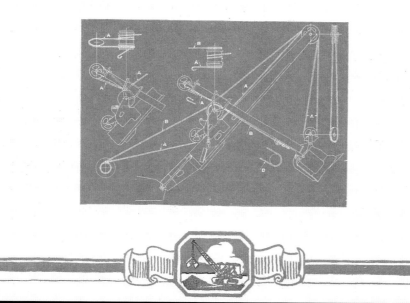

What really made a Northwest a "Northwest"? The patent that chief engineer Paul Burke is credited for in 1926 that set Northwest apart all other shovel manufacturers was "cable crowd". It was a simple, rugged and efficient means to move and crowd out a shovel's dipper stick through a cut of material, by using the tension at the end of the hoist cable. This page from Northwest literature describes the feature. Producing more yardages an hour, a Northwest front shovel had very few competitors.

The redesigned front shovel was first offered on the older Model 104 and 105 machines. The twin dipper sticks were placed on the outside of the boom; this arrangement gave a greater resistance to twisting while digging. Booms were still of riveted construction. Sway braces at the base of the boom are seen. Note also the operator has a seat. This was an industry first for Northwest, a simple solution to relieve the fatigue of long days of standing and throwing levers.

Contrasts in both loading machines and the hauling methods: top picture, an open-sided Model 104 with upgraded shovel front loads a contemporary Best crawler tractor with two wagons, and the lower photograph, a steel cab Model 105 is in stark contrast loading the fleet of mule-drawn wagons.

The contrast in machines: a wooden cab Erie Type B steam-powered shovel is seen here paired up with a steel cab, gasoline-powered Northwest Model 105 with the earlier version of front shovel. Both are working on a road improvement job. Gasoline power eliminated the water and coal requirements of the steam-powered machines. Could the operator of the Erie be a little jealous? He is still forced to stand all day to perform his task, but the Northwest operator has a seat all day.

A steel cabbed Model 105 loads rail hopper cars. The machinery house appearance of an enclosed Northwest represented quite a handsome machine for the day.

A factory steel sided Model 104 equipped with a gantry and clamshell working for T.J. Forschner Contracting Co. of Chicago Illinois. Northwest did offer both the Model 104 and 105 with a gantry option when heavier and longer lifting capacities were required of the customer.

Previous page: Two Model 105's with fully-enclosed machinery houses; the top dragline has the factory supplied style while the bottom crane appears the have homemade corrugated steel panels installed for the protection and comfort of both machine and operator.

Dig, cut, and haul: what couldn't a Northwest do? Well maybe not cut but given the opportunity and time Northwest's chief engineer Paul Burke might have patented an attachment that could have done just that. A very large sector of Northwest sales in the beginning years was to the lumber industry.

Following page: A Model 105 shovel in the top view and a Model 104 shovel in the bottom view; both employed by Merriel & Ring Lumber Company of Pysht, Washington. Pysht is a little village located in the upper portion of the Olympic Peninsula of Washington, an early 20th century heavy timber production area for the United States.

Stump control in this photograph seems to be the order for the day. Dual crowd not only helped with dirt and rock, but rooted stumps were not a match for a Northwest.

The same Model 104 shovel as the proceeding page but the terrain now has been modified with skillful operation and rugged machinery.

"Let's take a break"; these fine gentlemen in the employment of The Miller Logging Company of Seattle, Washington take a minute out of their busy day to pose for a photographer. Surely even operating a new Northwest Model 104 shovel with all its new creature comforts would require a little downtime. Especially this early version that was lacking the operator's seat.

A close-up view of the happy crew.

Two views of rail transported Model 104 shovels. Often rail delivery was the only practical option to place a piece of equipment back into heavy timber country. The above photograph is an outtake shot taken from a series of photographs for the cover of the last issue of The Northwest Exhaust dated November- December 1927. The Exhaust as it was known in company circles was Northwest's first published promotional magazine it would be replaced by larger formatted *Material Handling Illustrated* in early 1928.

A fine detailed photograph of an early Model 104 shovel working for Siler Logging Company of Everett, Washington.

A close-up view of the above model 104 shovel, we wondered how "Rover" likes a Northwest?

Pioneering work for big timber harvest is essential to the success of the operation. This series of photographs show the beginning and finished product to such an operation. The establishment of a well graded road could mean the difference in a good profit margin or loss.

Chapter two

"The Second Generation Machines"

The mid 1920's saw several significant changes occur at Northwest Engineering. The most sweeping was the change in ownership. The Barkhausen brothers were coerced out of their ownership of the firm by then company Secretary and Treasurer Louis E. Houston in late 1925. This inclusive change would lead to the establishment of corporate and sales offices located in Chicago headed up by Houston as the president and C.R Dodge as the vice president of sales. The factory at Green Bay would now be managed by Miss. B.E. Campbell. Miss Campbell would primarily run the front offices while each manufacturing department would be overseen by its own manager. A phone call or two per the work day was the routine for years between C.R. Dodge with Houston, (sometimes with the latter just listening in) and the factory management. This was done to ensure that production and orders were kept on schedule. Very rarely was Paul Burke, now vice president of engineering, ever a part of these daily meetings. Burke had complete autonomy over his department and his charge of engineers. Houston would leave the engineer and his department to self-govern for unknown reasons. It would be in this environment that Paul Burke could create new machinery for the ever changing material handling world.

Building upon the successes that the Model's 104 and 105 brought, Burke and his staff set about designing what would become known as "the second generation machines." in the latter half of 1925 and the beginning of 1926. They began on the lower end of the capacity range, machines in the half to three quarter cubic yard class. These sizes had begun to be manufactured by a number of competitors to Northwest and it made economic sense to the company to enter this class market. Since these were new classes and re-engineering to downsize was not a practical avenue to take, many new advances had occurred since the first generation machines had been introduced. Burke also went to the end user of the product, the owners and the many contractors who had purchased the earlier units, asking what and where the product could be improved and he listened.

Starting at the most logical point, the travel base, he redesigned from the ground up producing a rock solid platform to place the rest of the machine on. For the next sixty years the features in the travel base of a Northwest machine remained virtually unchanged. Heavy cast side rail frames along with a cast travel gear case being tied together with two very thick cross I-beams. Around all this ran tumbler shoes of a self- cleaning design driven by chains and sprockets.

Next to come would be the upper rotating base of a new fully enclosed design with ready access to all the machine's vital operating areas. Many customers liked the openness of the Model 104 and 105 for serviceability, but not so much when operating in inclement weather in the early machines, with their open-sided cabs and roll-down side curtains. The second generation machines now offered a fully-enclosed steel machinery house, with protection for the operator and machinery. The new lines of the house would have the boxy look of the period along with large paned glass front and side windows for the operator's vision and comfort. Gone too, would be the wooden planked floors of the first generation, now heavy gauge steel flooring was used. Ample thought was given by Burke for serviceability of the machines with sliding panels and doors at every major service point.

The second generation machine attachments were all of the standard types of the day, a Northwest could be factory equipped as a lift crane, a duty cycle crane, a shovel, a pullshovel or a skimmer-scoop. Along with these universal attachments, Northwest would offer customer requested or required modifications to the accessories and machines themselves. A very large portion of company revenues during the mid to late 1920's were obtained through these special "one-offs". In some cases, a full production run of a unique machine was required by a customer. For example, many railroads had Model 2's or Model 3's modified for a specific task. Also, a number of Northwest shovels found themselves digging in very low headroom, such as in tunnel construction. The dipper shovel mucker was a big seller during this time, most notably in the mid- range classes where size and power was needed and shorting the boom height got the job done.

All of the second generation machines from Northwest shared the same design criteria from the half yard Model 2 right on up through the final model in the series, the two yard Model 8. These sophomore offerings from Northwest Engineering Company would continue to cement the reputation that begun with the creed from H.G. and L.H. Barkhausen along with their engineering prodigy Paul Burke that was;

"To build a machine for service and not for sale"

Northwest Model 2

Produced from 1927 to 1941, ½ cubic yard capacity, 12000 lbs. lift capacity @ 12ft radius, 37000 lbs. working weight, with gasoline and electric power options.

A Model 2 shovel sequence shots, at a 1/2 cubic yard rated, capacity the Northwest Model 2 would be the smallest class production machine until the introduction of the third generation Model 15 rated at 3/8ths of a cubic yard a few years later.

Two more Model 2's outfitted with front shovels working in open pits with rail road hauling apparatus.

Two Model 2's in tropical conditions. The upper unit uses a peel clam TO clean out a swampy lagoon while the lower loads out sugar cane for the Kokaha Sugar Company located on the island of Kauai in the Hawaiian Islands.

Another specialized Model 2 crane. This longer gooseneck boom is well suited for the task at hand of loading and off-loading steel panels for the Midland Steel Products Corporation of Detroit Michigan. Many Model 2's found work as yard cranes, as their size and nimbleness made them ideally suited to provide fast service for waiting customers.

Previous page: Two Model 2's outfitted with special stub arch crane booms. This style boom fitted to a small Model 2 was ideal for loading dock work at rail terminals with low overhead conditions. No doubt swinging a load over the head of the man in the lower picture would highly be frowned upon in today's industrial settings.

Model 2's outfitted with the skimmer scoop attachment. The skimmer scoop came late to Northwest, only after seeing the success that other manufactures were having with the sales of these grading implements did the company set about developing their own version of the attachment.

Two photographs depicting the different stick arrangement when a skimmer scoop was switched over to pullshovel duties. The upper photograph is was the original fully reeved cable setup, while the lower photograph illustrates the newer, more robust design, with a roller chain.

Two photographs depicting the revised Model 2 pullshovel in action. Note the roller chain activated by the hoist cable block, and the generally heavier construction of the attachment, especially the upper boom head, tubular stick and pitch braces on the bucket.

Yet another variation of the Model 2 pullshovel. Note the slightly different design of the boom head and hoist arrangement, as compared to the photographs shown on the previous page. A clamp-on head has been attached to the boom head. A roller chain is still used in this design.

Two photographs depicting a Northwest in big timber country. Already, Northwest's were proving themselves as sturdy, reliable machines in the back country. This one, with an improvised timber boom loads logs.

Two sequential photographs of the machine previously illustrated sets logs on the waiting truck.

Two more views of the previous Model 2 loading out for Mount Emily Lumber Company of Le Grande, Oregon in 1937.

Northwest began to offer truck mounted equipment in the mid-1930's. The company only mounted the lower capacity units on customer supplied carriers such as this Mack tandem chain drive AC model above. Heavy factory modification was required to the chassis for these installations.

Northwest Model 3

Produced from 1927 to 1941, ¾ cubic yard capacity, 18,000 lbs. lifting capacity @ 12ft. radius, 44,000 lbs. working weight, with gasoline and electric power options.

A Model 3 shovel shown loading a rail mounted bucket loader for a brick clay operation.

A more detailed photograph of the previous Model 3 and the rail mounted bucket loader with its low sided side dump hopper cars.

A Model 3 outfitted with a clam doing a basement excavation. Note the open cab early dump truck. Scenes like this were common sight during the late 1920's in America; the urban build-up across the country was unlike any other decade preceding. Much of the construction activity was due to the advances of such machinery that Northwest and other manufactures were now producing. No more mass armies of manpower needed to dig a foundation or excavate a trench.

Previous page: Two wet Model 3's, up to their knees in muddy, and wet underfoot conditions. Obviously their operators had enough confidence in their machines' ability to negotiate such difficult and less-than-ideal environments.

A Model 3 crane working in an oil drilling operation. The construction and lumber industry was not the only trades to take advantage of new mobile lifting power.

Two Model 3 cranes equipped as cane loaders working in the Hawaiian Islands. Northwest established a very long relationship with sugar cane plantation owners in the early 1920s and continued this right on through the entire existence of the company. Many Northwests were seen working in the island chain on plantations 40 to 60 years after their initial delivery.

A Model 3 in the service of the Public Service Company of Northern Illinois hoisting a spool of cable.

Previous page: Model 3's loaded in gondola cars for rail maintenance work. Railroads were another industry strongly catered to by Northwest.

An extremely rare Model 3 outfitted with what would be known today as a zero tail swing option. Many of these units were supplied to the Pennsylvania Railroad for such operations as ballast placement on twin track rail heads where plenty of clearance was needed for the oncoming train traffic.

A Model 3 with just a shovel boom is set up at the Green Bay factory on an inclined ramp for brake testing on a 36% slope.

A Model 3 outfitted with the universal skimmer/scoop- pullshovel attachment .This unit is carrying the earlier, and rather unusual-looking, cable reeved pullshovel stick. Note the ground man with a story pole to check trench depth, a common practice in an era prior to lasers and auto grade instrumentation.

Previous page: Two views of a Model 3 skimmer owned by David Richards & Sons of White Plains, New York.

Northwest Model 4

Produced from 1930 to 1941, 1 cubic yard capacity, 30,000 lbs. lift capacity @ 12ft. radius, 62,000 lbs. working weight with gasoline and electric power options.

A Model 4 equipped with the rack-less rope crowding front shovel, the latest in face loading technology of the day. This particular machine was outfitted with an extended hi-front boom of either a homemade or aftermarket variety, but it appears to have the standard length twin dipper sticks.

Another Model 4 shovel working in Lexington, Kentucky for the Central Rock Company. Note the early Koehring Dumptor front discharge hauling unit.

This Model 4 shovel loads a Mack AC chain drive dump truck equipped with an earliest form of dump body hoist, a cable hoist mounted between the cab and bed, powered by the truck's power take-off. Both units belong to Kaufman Brothers of Northport, New York.

A Model 4 shovel with the factory hi-front option is working on the Big Four Roundhouse expansion in Cincinnati, Ohio. The contractor was Walsh Construction of Davenport Iowa. Note the difference in a Northwest supplied hi-front shovel boom as opposed to the unit on page 88. The truck is a Ford Model T with a Heil dump box.

A Pennsylvania Rail Road Model 4 on a drop side flatcar equipped with a boom and a clam appears to be depositing pieces of unused rail in their maintenance yard.

Following page: Model 4 skimmer on an urban street renovation project of the 1930's in Boston, Massachusetts for Karen Brothers. These sequential photographs show the digging and truck load out operation of a machine equipped as a skimmer-scoop quite well.

A very unusual but handy application for a Northwest. This Phelps Dodge Corporation gantry mounted Model 4 pullshovel at their Douglas Arizona facility is evening out a copper ore filled gondola cars for transport. The Model 4 was the first machine of the second generation machines that would be supplied with the very stout gooseneck boom equipped pullshovel. The Model 4 shared the same capacity ratings as that of the first generation Model 105 so the same pullshovel front could be used on the newer machine.

Another unusual adaptation of the pullshovel attachment. This Model 4 working in Philadelphia for Mazzola and Morano in 1933 was equipped with an experimental design of Paul Burke's that utilized a completely different geometry to cushion the shock of a fully-extended dipper stick, using the tensioned hoist cable. This version never went into full production.

Model 4 equipped with a homemade twin timber boom working for Algoma logging of Algoma Oregon in 1937. A Hyster logging arch with logs has just arrived at the loading site.

Following page: A Kinzua Pine Mills Company Model 4 easily stacks logs with its homemade timber boom.

Another Model 4 working for the Kinzua Pine Mills Company has been supplied with an early version of a heel boom for logging. Logging in the Pacific Northwest in the summer of 1937, many Northwest machines found little rest during the summer months.

Northwest Model 5

Produced from 1930 to 1941, 1 ¼ cubic yard capacity, 34,000 lbs. lift capacity @ 12ft. radius, 68,000 lbs. working weight with gasoline and electric power options.

A Model 5 shovel outfitted with a factory supplied hi-front shovel digging a basement excavation in Minneapolis, Minnesota for L.O. Danlquilt Construction Company. Note the sidewalk superintendents. The truck is a Mack AC chain drive with a Heil dump box.

Two views of a standard equipped Model 5 shovel loading out Caterpillar 60's pulling different crawler dump wagons.

Two nice close-up photographs detailing the Model 5 shovel. The machine is owned by Dan O'Connell's & Sons General Contractor of Holyoke, Massachusetts.

Model 5 shovels working for the Canisteo Cliffs Mining Company of Ishpeming, Michigan. The locomotive appears to be Baldwin-Hamilton 2-4-2. In the photograph below, note the loaded out rail cars on the trestle in the background.

Two views of one of Malby & Fowler's Model 5 working near St. Paul, Minnesota loading side dump rail cars. This is not a mining operation being performed, but rather a contract to widen the rail bed for an additional parallel track.

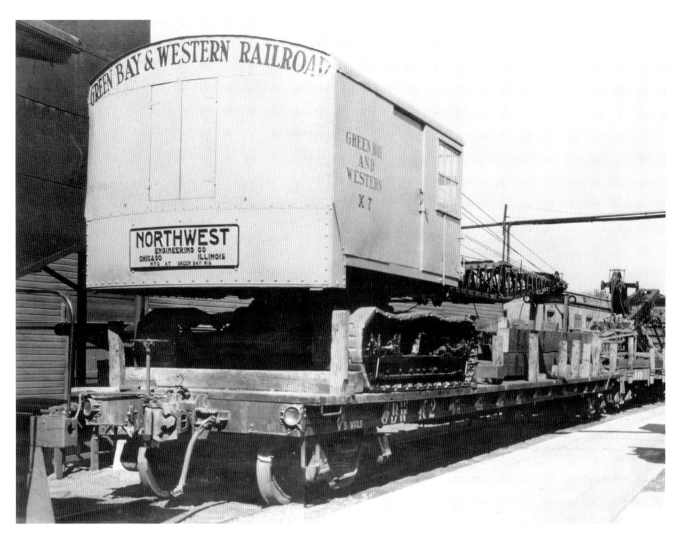

A Model 5 owned by Carmine Brothers equipped with a boom and clamshell doing a trench excavation and loading on occasion what appears to be a special narrow gage rail setup for the particular job.

Previous page: Many railroads bought Northwests for roadbed maintenance and various other duties. The photograph above shows a new Model 5 going into service for the Green Bay & Western as a wrecking train. The Model 5 outfitted with a clam in the bottom photo is doing culvert construction for the Foley Bothers Company of New York City.

Not only were shovels used in an urban setting for work but also out in the wilderness for logging applications. This Model 5 owned by Bloedel, Stewart & Walsh of Vancouver, British Columbia is being utilized for log skidding.

A Model 5 dragline working for El Oro Dredging Company of Maryville, California in 1939. The unit is loading a very rickety sluice built for gold mining.

Another Model 5 doing dragline work for Panob Gold Dredging Company of Loomis, California in 1940. This Model 5 is loading a much more durable portable sluice for gold mining mounted on free- wheeling crawlers and pulled by a Cletrac crawler tractor.

A Model 5 equipped with a hammerhead crane boom is working on a dirigible hanger at Wheeler field near Chicago, Illinois for The Austin Company.

Another Model 5 for The Austin Company with a hammerhead crane boom sets a steel truss on a more conventional hanger at Wheeler Field. Where are the brain buckets (hardhats) in these last two photographs?

This Green Bay & Western railroads Model 5 has a unique pile-driver attachment working off a flatcar; most likely setting new pile columns for a trestle repair.

Northwest Model 6

Produced from 1930 to 1980, 1 ½ cubic yard capacity, 38,000 lbs. lift capacity @ 12ft. radius, 72,500 lbs. working weight with gasoline, diesel and electric power options. The Northwest Model 6 and its line of variants had the distinction of being the longest produced model in the entire Northwest line.

This Nello L. Teer Model 6 loads an Athey crawler dump wagon. Nello Teer was one of North Carolina's largest road building contractors. A Model 6 had the right power and reach to make fast work of excavating a roadbed.

A special order tunnel mucking Model 6 shovel employed by Rusciano &Son of New York City. Low head room and big volume material moving was the issue here on this job. This particular shovel was not in a tunneling excavation but rather loading out stored material from a bunker with a low overhead.

This Model 6 pullshovel belonging to Henry W. Horst Company of Philadelphia and Buffalo performs trenching for an urban sewer project.

Previous page: Two profile views of a Merrill-Ring Lumber Company of Seattle Washington Model 6 shovel cutting in a logging road. Thanks to Northwest's excellent sales force in the Pacific Northwest the company enjoyed a very prosperous position in the timber industry throughout its entire life.

A Model 6 dragline loads out rail dump cars for List Construction Company of Kansas City, Missouri. It is very surprising how long it took diesel power to augment rail power; clearly here steam power is still the motive power for rail hauling.

Ferd J. Roberts Contractors of Burlington, Wisconsin uses a Model 6 for pile-driving on a rail stabilization job.

Heavy timber was not problem for this Model 6 owned by W. G. Robinson working near Mount Shasta, Califorina.

Northwest Model 7

Produced from 1930 to 1943, 1¾ cubic yard capacity, 40,000 lbs. lift capacity @ 12ft. radius, 75,000 lbs. working weight with gasoline, diesel and electric power options. Only offered with a pull shovel or lattice boom options.

Penton & Martins Construction Company of Florala, Alabama uses a Model 7 equipped as a dragline to load out clay on what appears to be a very rickety rail hauling operation.

M.Pontarell of Chicago Illinois with their Model 7 pullshovel loads out a chain drive Mack AC dump truck. The Model 7 pullshovel would be the largest trench digging machine offered in Northwest's second generation of machines. An easily recognizable feature to a Model 7 pullshovel was that the attachments stick differed from the smaller gooseneck equipped models in the second generation line. The pitch brace is located to the back side of the stick. The stick itself has a cambered design along with a much improved bucket sporting a transition curvature from the bottom to back enabling much better discharge of materials. Paul Burke and his staff were always evolving their designs.

Dowdle Brothers Company of Chicago Illinois uses a Model 7 pullshovel to perform some rail cleanup duties in a mining operation that is still using an antiquated steam powered rail mounted half-swing shovel seen in the background. A pullshovel also found work in a mining operation pulling and setting rail sections as the load out operation shifted. This particular Model 7 has a shorter stick that was sourced from a Model 6 size pullshovel; note that the pitch braces are located on the front side of the main member, and the bucket is of the older square back variety.

This Model 7 crane with an extension jib in a very deep canal excavation is working for Northern States Contracting of St. Paul, Minnesota. Note in the foreground the sheaves and cables for the tether cable system for cross pit delivery of building materials.

A partially obscured Model 7 performing clamming duties at the F. Hurlbutt Company coaling facilities in Green Bay, Wisconsin in 1935. These are the same coaling docks located on the east side of the Fox River that Northwest's very first machine, the experimental model, first worked at doing the same clamshell duties some 15 years earlier for its trial run. Owner Fredrick Hurlbutt Jr. was one of the original stock shareholders in Northwest Engineering Works when H.G and L.H. Barkhausen decided to change manufacturing direction from building tugboats to building gasoline powered crawler propelled full-revolving material handling equipment. Mr. Hurlbutt undoubtedly must have been happy with the trials; Northwests remained in his operation until the company changed ownership in 1986 and even then the machines at the facilities would not be phased out for many more years.

Northwest Model 8

Produced from 1930 to 1943, 2 cubic yard capacity, 18,650 lbs. lift capacity @ 25ft. radius , 79,000 lbs. working weight with gasoline, diesel and electric power options. Only offered with a lattice boom for lifting, dragline or clamshell duties.

The largest in the Northwest line for what would be considered the second generation machines. The Model 8 was a fairly big rig in its day. This one is doing dismantling work for its owner, Bethlehem Steel Company of Bethlehem, Pennsylvania. Northwest would offer the Model 8 only as a machine with long boom capabilities.

A Model 8 outfitted as a dragline working for Pioneer Contracting Company is seen loading out a line of Euclid FDT bottom dump units in Dyersburg, Tennessee in May of 1940.

Another view of Pioneer's Model 8 dragline loading out Euclid FDT bottom dumps. A Model 8 could swing a 2 cubic yard capacity bucket, which made short work of loading out the standard size construction haulers of the day. Note the long crawler base of the unit making the Model 8 a very stable platform to work from. The other Northwest feature of prominence on the Model 8 was the exceptionally tall gantry to help reduce boom compression, a feature that Paul Burke patented some 19 years earlier with the Type M machines of the first generation.

Two close-up views of Pioneer's Model 8 dragline.

Another Bethlehem Steel Corporations Model 8 labeled "Erection Car No. 60" is setting heavy steel for a section of elevated railroad in New York City. All the Model 8's supplied to Bethlehem were later built units in the series that sourced their rearward extended gantries from the new Model 80's that were being introduced in the mid to late 1930s. This combination of gantry offered a taller and more setback point for the boom bridle and pendants enabling greater resistance to boom compression and thus increasing the boom angle for higher and heavier lifts. The Model 8 series would be a glimpse of things to come with one of the all-time great full-revolving machines ever produced, the Northwest Engineering Company's Model 80-D.

A factory promotional photograph taken from a 1930 Northwest "Prestige" series catalog shows the many style attachments that Northwest could offer on their machines. Having such versatility and workmanship along with good promotion and sales in a product would rightly help place the name of NORTHWEST ENGINEERING COMPANY at the forefront of their industry for years to come.

Appendix

Factory photographs and machine/ engine data information

The Northwest Engineering Company factory, located on the west bank of The Fox River in Green Bay Wisconsin. This view was taken across the river on a cold winter day during the early 1920s. The last tugboat berth (the alcove on the right) is being filled in for future plant expansion.

A close-up view of the above photograph a steel cabbed Model 104 crane is seen next to the rail siding.

The same view as the proceeding page, only at the end of the 1920s. The last remnants of the shipbuilding days are gone. The alcove that previously contained the tugboat berth has been filled in, and the entire plant has been completely renovated for the new manufacturing direction.

A close-view of the photograph above, with the many models of machines in various stages of completion in the yard. How only in a few short years machinery production has taken off.

Another view taken from across The Fox River, this time at river elevation. This photograph was taken in 1925 which shows a transitional stage in plant evolution from the previous two pages.

A close-up view of the photograph above with the proud name of Northwest Engineering Company prominently displayed on the ridgeline of the old Hartmann & Greiling boiler works building.

An interior view of the factory dated 1925. Northwest did not have a foundry of its own, and sourced its castings from outside suppliers.

The pictures on the previous page, along with the picture above illustrates various components being assembled at the Green Bay factory. In the top picture opposite are Model 104 or 105 cabbed machines in various states of assembly sit in line, with the crawlers and carbody closest to the viewer, the draw works next, and cabs furthest away. The lower picture shows workers sliding what looks like a drum assembly onto a shaft,, while the picture on this page shows the hrizontal reverse shaft with the swing/travel clutches and bevel gears being assembled.

Two interior views of the fabrication shops.

Model 104

MODEL 104 is similar in design to the Model 105, but offers the additional advantage of greater capacity and horsepower and the heavier construction necessary to the handling of larger loads.

Convertibility, steering, operation maintenance—these are all as easy on the Model 104 as on the smaller Northwests. In spite of its size and ability it is shipped on one flat car without dismantling and was the first machine of 1¼ cu. yd. capacity which could be shipped in this manner.

> **1¼ cu. yd. shovel**
> **15 ton crane**
> **1¼ yd. dragline**
> **with 40 ft. boom**
> **49-59 inch trench**
> **Pull-shovel**

Gasoline Motor Drive

The Model 104 machine is powered with a Twin City engine, having 7¼″ and 9″ stroke, developing 74 b. h. p. at 550 R. P. M. It is of the valve-in-head type.

Lubrication is secured by means of high pressure force feed to all bearings, through drilled crankshaft, and splash to cylinders and pistons. The lubricating system is composed of a high pressure, gear driven oil pump, self-cleaning intake screen, spring loaded by-pass of the piston valve type to regulate the pressure, oil gauge, and H. W. Twin Oil Filtrator. All of the oil delivered to the bearings must pass through this Filtrator, thus eliminating any possibility of sediment or dirt being pumped into the bearings. The valve actuating mechanism, rocker arms, push rods and their bearings are inclosed and are constantly lubricated from the main oil pressure supply system.

The cooling system is of the forced water circulation type, employing a large water pump. All parts of the combustion chamber and cylinder wall are liberally water-jacketed with special stress being laid on cooling of the valves. The system is provided with thermostatic temperature regulation in order that the engine will warm up quickly and be maintained at an efficient working temperature in the winter time. A liberal fan and radiator is used, insuring proper cooling under extremely high temperature climatic conditions.

Ignition is secured by a Bosch high tension magneto.

Carburetion is by means of a 2″ adjustable Stromberg carburetor. The intake air is drawn through a dual Air-Maze air cleaner, and the mixture of gasoline and air is held to an efficient working temperature by a specially designed S hot-spot.

Fuel is delivered through an extra heavy and durable vacuum tank, the fuel being filtered before it enters the vacuum tank.

Electric Motor Drive

Where electric motor drive is desired, it makes possible an exceedingly simple installation. Only one motor is required which drives the first reduction gear through a full universal joint, thus relieving the motor bearings of any loads due to misalignment resulting from wear or other causes.

Current is delivered to the travel base through suitable plug-in connections and is transmitted to the rotating base by means of a set of large collector rings. All wiring is in conduit.

There are a number of electric powered Northwests located in various parts of the country equipped both as cranes and shovels. Many of these machines are successfully handling tough rock digging with an economy that can not be equalled by any other form of power. They are however, limited in mobility which is so necessary to most installations.

Twin City 74 H.P.-7¼″x 9″ engine used on the Northwest Model 104—a slow speed heavy duty power plant.

Model 105

MANY of the features that other manufacturers have recently adopted have been used in Northwest Models 105 and 104 since the first Northwest was built. They long ago ceased to be an experiment.

The most important of these are listed below.

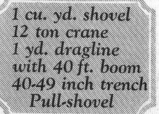

1 cu. yd. shovel
12 ton crane
1 yd. dragline
with 40 ft. boom
40-49 inch trench
Pull-shovel

1. The only thoroughly successful and practical steering device for a full revolving machine, controlled by a single lever at the operator's hand, and giving the great advantage of full traction on both sides of crawler while turning, as well as while traveling straight ahead.

2. The only machine that is absolutely easy of control. This is made possible by the Northwest "feather-touch" clutch control; the only device of its type which has a positive release and permits the feel of the bucket.

3. Extensive use of alloy steel and heat treated parts, giving long life under severe duty and at the same time holding the weight to a reasonable figure.

4. Powerful friction clutches throughout, with ample friction surfaces, resulting in cool running and infrequent adjustment.

5. Use of heavy type self-aligning ball bearings, making lubrication almost automatic—eliminating usual bearing troubles—resulting in material increase in net power delivered to the main drums for work by reducing friction losses.

6. Perfect drive from engine, resulting from use of helical cut-steel gears, mounted on ball bearings and running in an oil-tight housing. Silent operation of gears. Minimum friction loss.

7. Careful distribution of weight gives a maximum load carrying capacity per unit of total weight.

8. Powerful slow speed motor.

Wisconsin 66 H. P. engine used on Northwest Model 105—a slow speed heavy duty power plant. 4 cyl.—6"x7".

Gasoline Motor Drive

The Model 105 machine is powered with a Wisconsin engine, having a 6″ bore and 7″ stroke, developing 66 horse power at 825 R.P.M. It is of the valve-in-head type.

Lubrication is secured by means of high pressure force feed to all bearings through drilled crankshaft, and fresh oil lubrication is supplied to the cylinders and pistons by means of a Madison-Kipp high pressure Lubricator. The lubricating system is composed of a high pressure, gear driven oil pump, self-cleaning intake screen, spring loaded by-pass of the piston valve type to regulate the pressure, oil gauge and H. W. Oil Filtrator. All of the oil is filtered.

The cooling system is of the forced water circulation type and water pump. The system is provided with thermostatic temperature regulation in order that the engine will warm up quickly and be maintained at an efficient working temperature in the winter time.

Ignition is secured by a high tension Bosch magneto.

Carburetion is by means of a 2″ adjustable Stromberg carburetor with Air-Maze air cleaner and a specially designed S hot-spot.

Fuel is filtered before being delivered through an extra heavy and durable vacuum tank.

Electric Motor Drive

Electric power is furnished when desired. The installation is exceedingly simple. Only one motor is required for all operations. This drives the first reduction gear through a full universal joint, thus relieving the motor bearings of any loads due to misalignment resulting from wear or other causes.

The Model M on sewer work.

Type M — Dragline-Crane

The remarkable mobility of the Northwest dragline due to the patented steering device that delivers full power to both crawlers while turning as well as while going straight ahead made the Northwest virtually the standard of the drainage field.

The standard Models 104 and 105 answered the demand very satisfactorily, but there was also a place for a larger machine having the exclusive features pioneered by Northwest.

This place is filled by the Northwest Type M, a machine capable of handling a longer boom with greater stability. The Type M has all the valuable features of the Model 104. As a dragline it can be equipped with a 1 cu. yd. Class "C" Page drag-line bucket on a 50 ft. boom. This supplies the long reach so often necessary in clean-out and trench work.

As a crane the Type M has 11% greater capacity than the Model 104 (see specifications). When handling pipe it is possible, by using a 3-part line, to handle a 6-ton load at a 32-ft. radius with a 40-ft. boom.

The crawlers are long and wide, 16' 4" x 11' 6", providing a stable base that greatly offsets the tipping load. But in spite of its size the Type M can be shipped to practically any section of the country without dismantling.

The Type M is powered with a 4-cylinder Twin City gasoline motor of 7¼" bore by 9" stroke and develops 74 horsepower at 550 R. P. M.

NORTHWEST POWER PLANTS

Special attention has been given to Engines used on Northwest Equipment. At Green Bay, Wis., an engine laboratory is maintained that with few exceptions is larger than the laboratory of any engine manufacturer and is the only one maintained by a builder of shovels, cranes, draglines, pullshovels and skimmer-scoops.

Here engines of various makes are constantly under test, also oils and fuels, not only from our own country, but from all over the world, undergo examination and test.

The following section is devoted to the description and illustration of this laboratory and the power plants on Northwest Equipment.

ENGINEERING RESEARCH GUARANTEES QUALITY

The corner of the laboratory shown above is devoted to carburetion testing and research. Here the efficiency and exact performance of any type of carburetion under every sort of condition can be accurately determined. Glass windows enable engineers to watch the mixture and highly accurate meters enable exact determination of efficiencies.

The chemical laboratory shown below is equipped with elaborate apparatus for examining lubricating oils and the chemical qualities of metals and materials which go into Northwest machines. Here chemists can determine the comparative values of different kinds of fuels and lubricating oils so that Northwest users can be advised of what to use in order to get maximum efficiency and long life from their equipment. Much research work on the difficult problem of crank case dilution has been done here.

The engines used on Northwest equipment are not ordinary stock engines. Contrary to usual practice they incorporate many special features developed in the research laboratory of the Northwest Engineering Co. and are built to rigid specifications laid down by the Northwest engineering staff after the most careful testing and experimenting to find the power plant most perfectly adapted to the job.

The $70,000 Northwest engine research laboratory is more completely equipped than that of many motor manufacturers and Northwest is the only manufacturer of material handling equipment to maintain a complete laboratory for engine testing and research. Scientific apparatus and complete testing equipment enables engineers who specialize on engine design to check every detail of engine performance.

Improvements and experimental designs of many kinds are constantly being investigated in an effort to provide the best possible power plant. No detail of carburetion, lubrication, ignition or cooling is left to guess work on the Northwest engine. Every Northwest accessory as well as the complete power plant is constantly being subjected to searching tests in order to guarantee satisfactory performance and to point the way to further improvements.

This 100 H.P. electric dynamometer testing plant is where Northwest engines are put to the acid test by hours of running under all kinds of load and operating conditions. Here a Wisconsin engine is shown hooked up ready to run for testing. At the left will be seen a Twin-City engine ready to be hooked up; at the left above is the control panel.

Typical recent developments of such research work are the Variable Speed Engine and the Accelerator Control, the design of which was worked out in the laboratory by means of long and exhaustive tests before it was finally adopted as a feature of Northwest machines.

The importance of this laboratory to the Northwest user can hardly be overestimated for it gives him the assurance that improvements, experiments and untried features will not be tested out in the field at the owner's expense. With the aid of this complete laboratory Northwest engineers can submit every part of the machine and every new feature to accurate scientific tests that are far more severe than any condition the machine will ever be called on to meet after it is in the owner's hands and out on actual service. No new feature is ever adopted on the Northwest machine until it has proven its merit in the acid test of this laboratory where guess work can be eliminated.

Equipment for testing engine accessories such as magnetos, radiators, thermostats, pumps, etc., is shown below. Here a magneto can be put through tests which will show how it will stand up in the field. Sensitive apparatus is used to measure everything from the flow of gas to the carburetor to the flow of air through the radiator. Automatic recording apparatus makes actual test charts of the character of combustion in the cylinder, valve timing, ignition and many other factors.

POWER PLANTS— MODELS 2, 3 AND 4

The gasoline engines on Models 2, 3 and 4 are built by the Wisconsin Motor Company, but are of special design for the Northwest Engineering Company, embodying features developed in the Northwest laboratory. These special features have been incorporated to fit them to meet the severe and peculiar conditions imposed on a shovel or crane in service.

Changes in load requirements on engines in this service are extremely rapid. Any engine to be successful on a shovel or crane must be able to operate at no load or any load for an indefinite period, change from one load to another instantly without faltering and stand "drag-down-loads" without detonation or "ping." The special Northwest type of combustion chamber, a special form of overhead valve type which permits higher compression, is so successful in respect to this problem as to justify the sweeping statement that with ordinary gasoline as fuel, the engine may be operated under any practical combination of conditions as to load, speed or spark advance, without showing any detonation or "ping" whatsoever. This represents a distinct advance over the so-called L-head combustion chamber in respect to power developed, and assures an unusually large amount of power for a given piston displacement.

Special attention has been paid to the development of maximum torque at speeds substantially under the governed normal

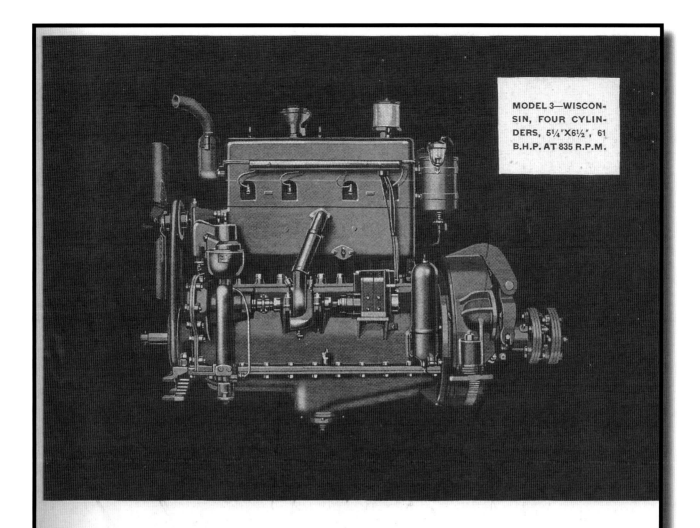

MODEL 3—WISCON-
SIN, FOUR CYLIN-
DERS, 5¼"X6½", 61
B.H.P. AT 835 R.P.M.

speed of the engine. This helps the engine to sustain "drag-down" loads without a flywheel of heavy proportions with its destructive effects. An engine really adapted to powering a crane or shovel requires a flywheel of only moderate weight.

The lubrication system is a high pressure feed system composed of a high pressure gear driven oil pump. It has adequate oil filters for the extraction of all sediment and other impurities. There is also a large area self-cleaning screen on the pump intake, an added insurance toward clean lubrication. A spring loaded by-pass of the piston type regulates the oil pressure and there is a suitable oil gauge. Particular attention has been given toward a crankcase cooling surface adequate to maintaining the crankcase oil at a proper temperature.

All the valve actuating mechanism, rocker arms, push rods and their bearings are fully inclosed and are constantly lubricated from the main oil pressure supply system. Baffles in the crankcase prevent the oil from shifting when swinging or working at an angle.

The cooling system is ample in all respects. It is of the forced circulation type and assures plenty of radiation and a water pump of large capacity. All parts of the combustion chamber and cylinder walls are water-jacketed with special attention to the valves.

The outlet from the water pump is at the top of the cylinders giving maximum cooling where cooling is most needed around the valves and combustion chamber, allowing the pistons to work in cylinder barrels at a reasonable temperature, resulting in better lubrication and lower engine friction and consequently less dilution.

Thermostatic temperature regulation insures rapid warming up and efficient operation even in cold weather.

MODEL 4—WISCONSIN, FOUR CYLINDERS, 6"X7", 75 B.H.P. AT 795 R.P.M.

The matter of carburetion on the Northwest is the result of constant tests and experiments over a long period of time in the Northwest engine laboratory. Carburetors on Northwest machines may be depended upon for accurate metering. Special means are employed for breaking up the fuel after it passes the carburetor. Proper heat control is provided so that under all weather conditions the proper manifold temperature with corresponding good fuel vaporization and distribution is assured. All fuel passes through a filter on the way to the vacuum tank and air cleaners assure effective cleaning regardless of the engine speed.

Ignition is secured by a high tension magneto with spark control.

Electric Motor Drive

Electric power is furnished, when desired, on all Northwests. Only one motor is required for all operations. This drives the first reduction gear through a full universal joint, relieving the motor bearings of any loads due to misalignment.

As in the gasoline machine there is only one motor on the Northwest when electrically powered. This eliminates the usual complications of three-motor operation and permits simple design. There is no mass of complicated wiring or control devices. You are able to shake the dipper with the usual violence of the gasoline machine.

The economy of the electric power plant is recognized everywhere.

Its field of service lies in clay pits, quarries, building supply yards and industrial plants where traveling is over short distances and not of great importance. Suitable plug-ins can be arranged on the installation so that traveling can be done over an area restricted only by the length of cable and the number of outlets.

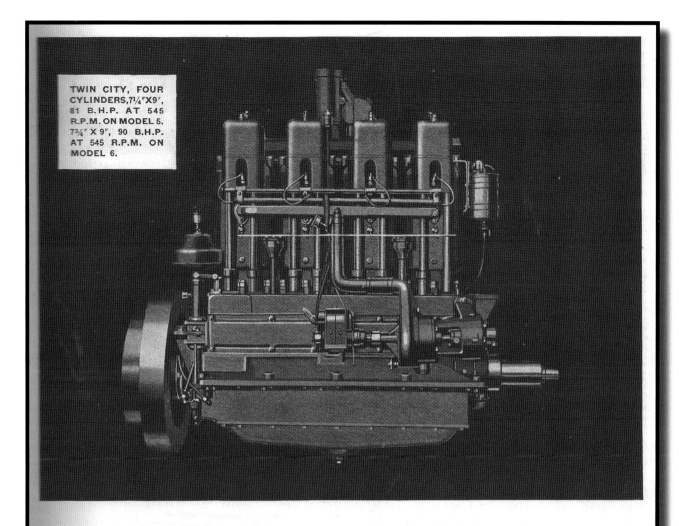

TWIN CITY, FOUR CYLINDERS, 7¼"X9", 81 B.H.P. AT 545 R.P.M. ON MODEL 5. 7¾" X 9", 90 B.H.P. AT 545 R.P.M. ON MODEL 6.

POWER PLANTS—
MODELS 5 AND 6

The gasoline engines on the Models 5 and 6 are built by the Minneapolis Steel & Machinery Co.

The 7¾" x 9" engine on the Model 6 is the largest engine offered on any crane or shovel of equal capacity, which means that it operates at the slowest speed of any such power plant.

A prominent characteristic of these engines is the heavy and rugged construction and liberal proportioning of all parts.

Years of service on many hundreds of Northwests have established a wonderful reputation for reliability and ability to "hang on"

under the severest conditions of overload.

These engines are of the valve-in-head type. All valve mechanism is inclosed. Lubrication is by high pressure, gear driven pump. All lubricating oil passes through an H. W. Filtrator. In spite of the high torque developed, the operation is free of any objectionable degree of detonation.

Cooling is by forced circulation with special stress laid on the cooling of the valves. A thermostatic temperature regulator assures quick warming up and proper operation under the extremes of climatic conditions. Ignition is by Bosch high tension magneto.

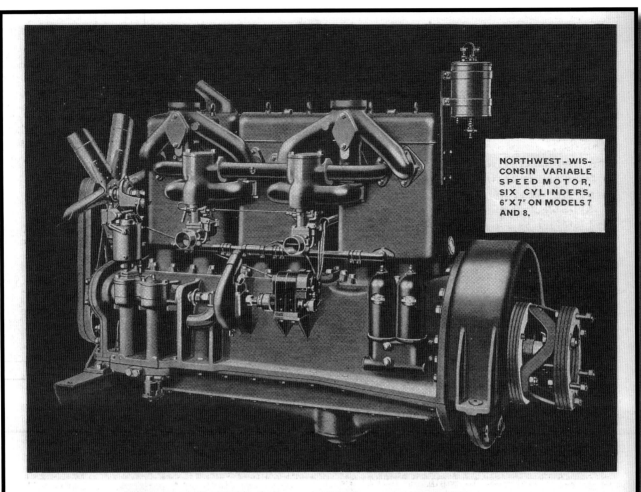

NORTHWEST - WIS-CONSIN VARIABLE SPEED MOTOR, SIX CYLINDERS, 6″ X 7″ ON MODELS 7 AND 8.

POWER PLANTS— MODELS 7 AND 8

NOTE: The Northwest Variable Speed Motor, Accelerator Controlled, is standard on Models 7 and 8 and can be supplied at extra cost on Model 6 in place of the regular Twin City.

The Northwest Variable Speed Motor, Accelerator Controlled, is the result of many months of laboratory research and experimentation followed by exhaustive tests in the field, and is the first fully flexible engine with accelerator control available for this type of machine. This engine is a radical departure from the fixed speed engines which have always been used and gives to the operator a power plant with motor car flexibility. It brings instant responsiveness to an increase in load or an increase in speed, and the variation in speed is 100% above the normal operating speed of the engine when considered as a governor controlled engine.

The maximum torque or pulling power occurs at a speed considerably under normal, giving maximum stability and freedom from stalling—and these things are accomplished with good fuel economy.

The motor is a Wisconsin with a 6″ bore and 7″ stroke, which incorporates a new design of combustion chamber, developed entirely in the Northwest experimental laboratories. This combustion chamber, a special form of the overhead valve type, represents a distinct advance over the so-called L-head combustion chamber in respect to power and freedom from detonation. It makes possible for the first time an engine which will pull perfectly at any speed between 450 and 1200 R.P.M., deliver the full power which should be available at that speed, and at the same time respond reliably to sudden changes in speed.

A governor is installed which permits it to be operated in the conventional manner as a fixed speed engine, if desired. But when hand control is desirable, full manual control of engine speed is obtained by the movement of a simple lever.

The variable speed feature requires almost no effort to actuate and permits the operator to keep his feet on the brake pedals and his hands on the operating levers while controlling the whole range of the engine speeds. The hand grip portion of the lever controlling the travel, swinging clutches is pivoted and can be moved to the left and right. In the vertical or normal position the engine operates as a governor controlled power plant, moving the lever to the right or left, reducing or increasing the speed. This method of controlling speeds is far superior to that method employing change of gears. It permits the maintenance of the Northwest policy of simplicity of design and brings not merely a choice of *two-travel speeds* but an *infinite number varying from the lowest to the highest*—and the change of speed applies to every operation and not to travel alone as is the usual case.

In the gear method of speed change, the use of a higher gear ratio results in a loss of effective torque and a proportionate reduction in tractive effort. This is not the case with the Northwest Variable Speed Motor, thus in climbing grade the tractive effort is not materially reduced when the higher speeds are used.

The overall result that every prospective purchaser should keep in mind is that the speed of every operation is increased, giving a considerable advantage. On hoisting or swinging operations where high speed is desirable the operator can open up the engine to top speed at the touch of the finger just as with the steam machine, thus saving considerable amounts of time. On crane and clam-

shell work where extremely sensitive handling is necessary the load or bucket can be handled very accurately with a low speed, and as soon as the load is picked up or the bucket ready to close, the throttle may be opened and maximum speed used to close the bucket or to hoist and swing.

In some classes of digging, a dragline bucket will settle into the material better if the first few feet of the loading is performed at slow speed. The operator can then accelerate and complete the loading operation at higher speed.

In field tests this engine has proven itself capable of delivering from 15 to 20% more when the accelerator control is used than when the engine is permitted to operate on the fixed speed governor controlled. This is a very substantial increase in gross output. We therefore urgently recommend that where consideration is being given to the use of fuels heavier than gasoline, the prospective purchaser give serious thought to the question whether the increase in gross income possible with this power plant will not outweight any theoretical saving in fuel cost.

In design and construction this engine is on a par with all Northwest power plants. Particular attention is called to the freedom from vibration, quietness and general operating smoothness. The heavy crankshaft is bedded in bearings supported by an unusually heavy and rigid crankcase.

Lubrication is through a high pressure system. All oil passes through a filtrator that catches all dirt. Valve actuating mechanism, push rods, rocker arms and their bearings are fully enclosed and are constantly lubricated from the main oil supply.

The cooling system is of the forced circulation type. All parts of the combustion chamber and cylinder are water-jacketed with special attention to the valves. Ignition is secured by high tension magneto with spark control. Fuel is filtered before delivery to the vacuum tank.

FOR THE PURPOSES OF ILLUSTRATION THE NORTHWEST TWIN CITY OIL ENGINE IS SHOWN.

NORTHWEST OIL ENGINE

The operation of the Northwest Oil Engine is similar to the gasoline motor. It has all the essential features: spark plugs, magneto, everything your operator understands. It brings gasoline motor dependability, presenting the advantage of greater simplicity than the high compression engine and complete freedom from the high gas pressures essential to the operation of that type, yet brings the low cost operation which comes with burning fuels of a lower grade (lower distillation range) than gasoline, i. e., fuels of a distillation range having an end point of distillation 550-600° F. (288°-316° C.)

The Standard Oil Company's (of Indiana) "Stanolind" is a typical satisfactory fuel for these engines. Similar fuels may be obtained from the Shell Oil Company (No. 1 Stove Oil) and also from the Sinclair Oil Company and many others.

The Northwest Oil Engine eliminates the constant theft of fuel which many contractors find is a big item. It is not necessary to buy in carload lots as the extensive use of oils for household fuel makes it possible to secure a suitable fuel practically anywhere by tank wagon delivery. In remote sections where this is not possible the cost of fuel haulage is greatly reduced.

The essential features of the Oil Engine are: (1) The proper development of carburetor apparatus for low grade fuels resulting in accurate metering. (2) Adequate vaporization of the heavier fuels to permit clean burning under extremely varying conditions of load which are characteristic of crane and excavator operation. (3) A special combustion chamber shape which promotes clean combustion, together with the suppression of undue detonation and a special additional means for suppressing detonation. (4) A special means for the elimination of lubricating oil dilution which otherwise would accompany the use of fuels materially heavier than gasoline.

Starting from cold is accomplished by running the engine for a few minutes on gasoline for which a small tank is provided.

The Northwest Diesel Engine

AFTER five years of close observation of small Diesel engines, and after considerable study and experimentation, the Northwest Engineering Company offers a 4-cylinder full Diesel unit that is specially designed for use on excavating and material handling equipment. It is not merely a marine engine placed on a shovel, crane or dragline.

In the well-known true Diesel cycle, which has been successfully and widely used over more than two decades in large size engines, the fuel is injected into the combustion chamber with a jet of high pressure air. This serves to break up the fuel very finely thus making it more readily and completely combustible. With this method it was naturally very difficult to secure effective operation in small cylinder sizes. First, a high pressure air compressor—an expensive and troublesome affair—was necessary, and second, accurate metering was next to impossible.

There are on the market today many solid injection engines suitable for marine service but because no one has previously been able to accurately meter the small quantity of fuel necessary for small cylinders there were necessarily fewer than four cylinders in order to keep them as large as possible.

In other engines injection is accomplished by means of a troublesome pump operating at a high pressure of 3500 lbs. or more. They are bulky and the heavy masses of the reciprocating parts coupled with the fact that usually the cylinders are fewer than four in number results in falling considerably short of the relatively smooth operation to which the excavator and crane owner has become accustomed in the 4-cylinder gasoline engine. The rigid foundations met with in stationary service and the relatively solid foundations possible in marine installations cannot, of course, be realized in the overhung frames necessarily a part of the excavator or crane.

The method of injection used in this Diesel is the solution of the air injection problem. It brings the effectiveness of the air injection type minus the handicap of the air compressor and is without the high pressure pump and attendant difficulties of the solid injection type. It provides the Northwest with the simplest Diesel engine on the market.

The fuel pump is a self-contained unit, all mechanism being enclosed in a box filled with fuel oil. This serves the double purpose of lubricating the moving parts and causing all leaks from plunger and valves to drain back into the system, thereby preventing unsightly and wasteful fuel leaks.

Fuel is metered by individual pumps for each cylinder. The lift of the intake valves for each pump is directly controlled by the governor and varies in accordance with the load. From the pump, the fuel is piped to each injector by individual lines communicating with the fuel chamber in each injector at (m). A special cam on the cam shaft takes care of the plunger (n). At the lower end of the injector are two cone shaped cups opening through passages into the combustion chamber and to the plunger chamber directly above. The action is as follows: during the intake stroke the needle valve admits fuel to the cone shaped cup (g).

Note there is no direct connection between the space (k) below the ball check and the space (c) below the plunger. On entering the space (g) the fuel spreads over the entire bottom area and is heated by the heat of the cylinder which reduces its viscosity and prepares it for complete atomization. As there is insufficient air present in (c) to support combustion, ignition cannot take place. During the compression stroke air is forced up into (g) and (e) and helps to complete the preparation of the fuel. The heated compressed air passes up through the orifices into space (c).

A sharp, accurately timed return thrust of the plunger (a), taking place just before the compression stroke ends, injects the fuel and air through the spray nozzle into the combustion chamber in which, meanwhile, the pressure has risen to 500 pounds. With this rise in pressure has occurred a rise in temperature sufficient to ignite the fuel. This positively timed mechanical ignition is accomplished without the use of an injection pump, nor is a primary explosion depended on. The method is purely mechanical

Page fourteen

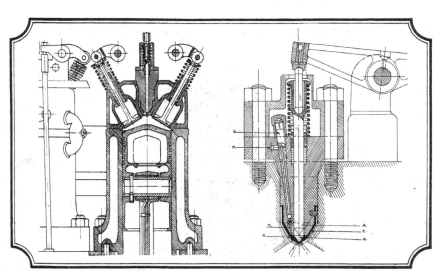

Cross Section of Diesel Engine Cylinder and Injector used on Northwest

and unusually simple, overcoming the problem of the trouble-causing high pressure pump and air compressor, yet approaching the effectiveness of atomization in the air injection type of Diesel engine. Because metering is accurate all limitation to the smallness of cylinders is removed and the use of 4 cylinders is permitted, which in turn brings well balanced operation largely free from the vibration always present in the three cylinder type. Because there *are* 4 cylinders, power impulses are closer together and pickup is quick allowing greater flexibility of control. Because of more perfect atomization and complete combustion *at all loads* combined with high compression, this Diesel burns a wider range of fuels than other small Diesels thus effecting the maximum in fuel economy. Without a question it is the simplest full Diesel used for powering shovels, cranes and draglines. Everything on the engine that ever calls for adjustment or examination is readily accessible and most of those are in separate units easily dismantled or replaced. The cylinders are cast separately. This permits the easy removal of any cylinder.

The crank-case is of unusually heavy and rigid section helping to eliminate vibration. The crankshaft is machined all over from a hammered forging, heat-treated. This assures strength, toughness and excellent working qualities. The pistons are exceptionally long and each one has seven rings. All crank shaft and connecting rod bearings are bronze backed babbitt lined. The connecting rod shank portion is a steel forging, the big end made of a split bronze casting (babbitt lined) being bolted to the main portion of the rod.

Lubrication is full pressure feed to all main and connecting rod bearings and to piston pins as well.

Cylinders are oiled from the same system so that a separate lubricator for them is not needed. Oil is circulated by means of a geared pump. The lubrication system is so arranged that the flow of oil is not interrupted when the machine is operating at an angle. Water is used for cooling and the water jackets never approach the boiling point. The exhaust manifold is water jacketed and there is no point on the engine except a short length of pipe up through the roof that reaches a temperature hot enough to burn one. Water is circulated through the radiator and cooling system by means of a centrifugal pump, gear driven from the cam shaft gear train.

The governor is of the spring loaded fly ball type, built integrally into the engine and gear driven.

All the air taken into the engine passes through an air cleaner and a large filter is provided for the fuel. The Diesel engine on the Northwest is started by compressed air and gives a practically instantaneous start from stone cold. No heating by torch, hot bulb, cartridge or similar device is necessary and there are no electrical devices on the engine.

For starting, a small air compressor driven by a small gasoline engine is provided. This charges a large storage tank. Twenty minutes operation will suffice to fill this tank, and one charge of the tank permits from 10 to 15 starts. Cold or wet weather will not affect the starting of the Northwest. It starts under all conditions even easier than a gasoline engine.

A fuel tank of 100 gallons capacity is provided. Under the great majority of conditions it is unnecessary to take on fuel oftener than twice a week—a feature worth considering where fuel must be hauled long distances.

And away they go...

A shipment of Model 2's loaded on flatbed rail cars headed to new customers.

The back insignia on a 1926 sales catalog.

THE END

For a more comprehesive history on Northwest Engineering Company, its Products, and key personel, the following title is available by the authors.

ISBN   9781494342012

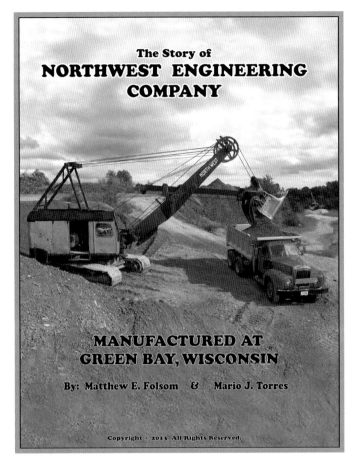

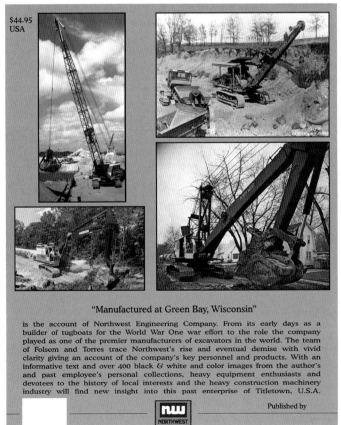

"Manufactured at Green Bay, Wisconsin"

is the account of Northwest Engineering Company. From its early days as a builder of tugboats for the World War One war effort to the role the company played as one of the premier manufacturers of excavators in the world. The team of Folsom and Torres trace Northwest's rise and eventual demise with vivid clarity giving an account of the company's key personnel and products. With an informative text and over 400 black & white and color images from the author's and past employee's personal collections, heavy equipment enthusiasts and devotees to the history of local interests and the heavy construction machinery industry will find new insight into this past enterprise of Titletown, U.S.A.

Published by

Scheduled for release next in this series by the authors is;

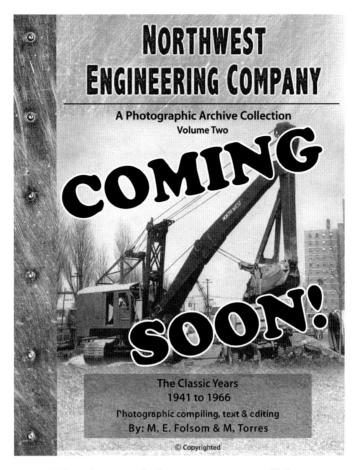

The last of this series will be;

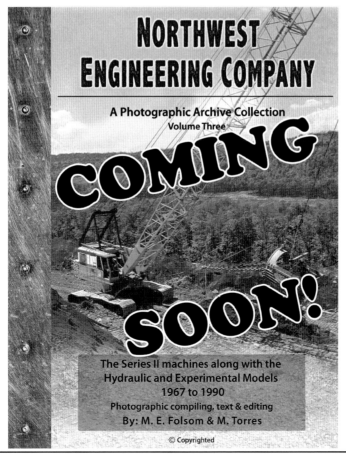